Dedicated to you.

Authors Note

Hello you!

This book of poems is a journey throughout my personal experiences and connection with all
beings. Each page provides a newfound prospective of life though playfully, powerful rhymes. Each poem holds a deeper meaning that can be understood by meditating on the profound meaning of the words
within the versus.
This book suggests that we are connected to all things in an intimate and eternal way, and explores what that means for us identifying self as an individual on this earth.

Allow yourself the opportunity to cry, smile, laugh and breathe easy as you immerse yourself in the world and words of One human to the next.

As you are reading the following pages and stumble upon one that strikes your core feel free to share a photo of your favorite page and tag me on instagram @Good.Vibes.Deliverry as I would love to acknowledge you and connect through the words.

Nonetheless I appreciate you investing into expanding your mind by sharing these mutually felt moments.

I love you, and wish you well on your journey

Discipline of the Law of One

In discipline lies in what we can understand as two
mediums. "Self" and "other self"

God   Ego

Our ego strives to stay constant.
Normal. Habitual.
Striving to stand out in every way.
Yet our true self, who is orchestrating all things,

God,
Is naturally
Light
Peace
Joy
Expanding
Unconditionally loving
One.

To let go of self and give freely
Is to experience all and receive all.

LET US BEGIN

Torn

They tell me to love all yet why do I feel so torn?
Perhaps the shedding of a skin
One of a kin
Dead.
To mourn the sin
That has been forgiven

Only Human

I tend
To hide
A way
Too scared
To bud
I give
With no expectation
to receive
"Alien"
To "Me"
All of humanity.

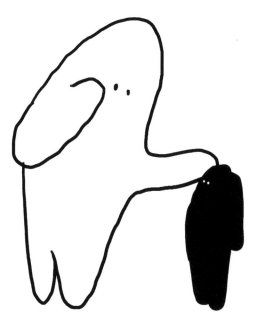

Pity

Self-pity
addictive
Destructive
Curiosity?
No sin
Forgive
Let go you see
The fruit has long been ate
From the knowledge tree.

The nature Of ME

I want to experience more of the pleasant joys of
nature in its raw peaceful beauty.
I am safe.
I am free.
To run
To cry
To yell
To be.
Wholly and impurely me.
And that could not make me more happy.

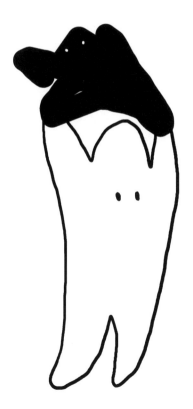

Invisible Feelings

Joy
Swells in me
Ever Growing
Peacefully.
A calmer mist
Dwells in me
Overflowing in a sea
We can only feel
But cannot see.

Experiment

Experience

I am here.
Where to next?
Changing the frequencies
Is like sending a text
What reply do you want?
only you can decide
In this place
There is no space
For ego or pride
    We   will   glide   from side
To side
Letting   go
               is part   of the ride.
So meet you back,   on the
other side.

Now

I expand
Focused
Attention
  NOW
Presence
Focused
Attention
  NOW
Only
Focused
Attention
  NOW
Here being in the moment of
Now.

Lead

I sometimes stop
and worry still
Yet I know it does no good
And can make me ill
Which makes me thank
the God above
 for sending forth this precious love
Leading me.
My Heart Is aligned
With My Soul
        Body
        And mind.
In each moment lays a tender moment
Gentle
Kind.
Holding my own one true core
of humankind

Finding Solace

In a shoelace
Binding strings of words
Lacing us together

When a turbulent train of thought
Leads me off my track
I take a moment to see where I've come or gone
And then change the direction
To what I want

And then

It's gone.

Connected Wonder

Peace
Together
The atomic
Chain
That loops
And spirals
The cells
Surround
Connected
To everything:
The air
The sea
The sky
The ground
It all comes back in
The beginning and
End
A spiraling circle
So large does it bend.

War

Surviving the
downfall
Creating new ways
To overcome a common error

If man was a mirror
The reflection of terror
Would cause him to stop.

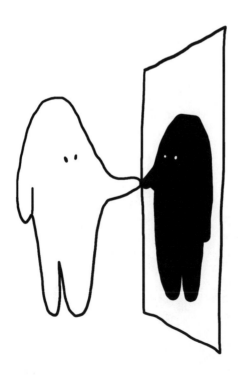

Sound

Yes.
I am
Full of Bright Light
Eating me alive
God
Will I survive?
Or be burned Alive?
In you I thrive
In love
You arrive.

Cannon Falling

Falling
Falling
Cannon balling
Big old splash
Waves will crash
Filled to the brim
Ready to swim
In the giant
Cup
I've landed in.

Rest

When you've been moving moving moving,
Moving naturally
Gaining more momentum
In the path of do and be
Be wary of the speed you
Find yourself at pace
Be cautious of the speeds where the rest is out of
place.
Remind yourself constantly
That this is not a race.
To give yourself the rest you need
At this time and place.

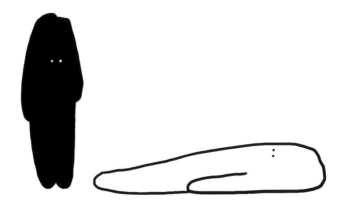

Chakra Rhymes

I feel Red to my roots
Green like trees in my heart that
grows a ripe orange for my tummy.
Blue for my throat that says "I am."
Yellow glows from my diaphragm
Purple sparkles in between my eyes.
And a magenta light shoots from the top of my head
into the skies.

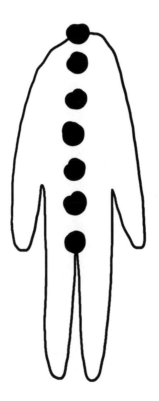

A Letter To All That Has.

Letting go
Letting go
Letting go.
Do you serve me? No.
Then let me go.
Let it flow
From my heart
To sky
I have let it all go
Without needing to try
All that does not serve me
Can now get up and fly
Away from my being
No longer with I
Thank you for fleeing
And releasing from me
Now I can sigh.

Good bye.

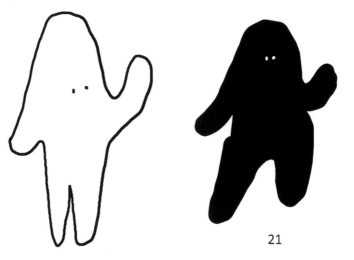

Vibration

How high does it go?
Higher than I know.
How to soar higher?
Flow
Allow
Trust
And know
Your vibration is much higher than this.
So let that low stuff go.
Smile
Gratitude. Thank you
Pleasure as pure as snow
Connected to up above
With this body down below.
Planting a seed of light
Watching it all grow.

Perception

You are not what I see
but what I feel
brought to reality
all I need is within me
Innerwork changes who I be

look again
different now
perceiving from my third eye brow
climbing up the ladder now
bird's eye view I can see what's true
and when I'm done I will climb down
To act accordingly and receive my crown

I seek the light

I seek to examine the darkness with love
Shining a kindness beam from above
Visions of the future
Filled with light and love

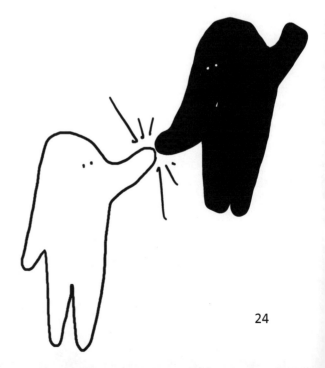

The sea of stress-free

Just a slight ocean breeze
Covering me in sunlight.
The waves greet me bye-bye
And offer a sigh
Of relief
To the grief
That's been set free
To just be.

To The Sleepers

I see you every day.
You are no different than me
Other than the words you say.
We come from the same one.
And though you sleep you do not lay
And don't understand the words you say
A scene brought up from your third eye— see!
Can you feel the energy?
I love you
Do you love me?

Bright side

There are two walls
That beckon me to see
One is bright light
The other is dark dreary
I walk in between
But I'll lean
On the brightest of walls
Cause I'm a sunbeam

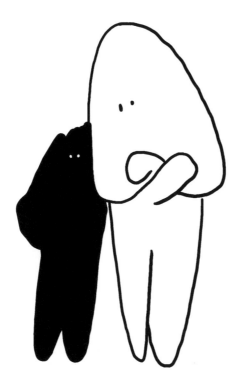

Guest

In your own body
Lies seeds of trees
Growing past your knees
Attracting honey bees
Pleasant breeze

Not here for permanent
Just here to see
Leaving a trail
So you know it was me

Spring

Tree
Grow
Bird Fly
Snow Go
Sun
Shine.

Crown

My crown
Weighs down
I frown
Take down
Don't drown
The sky
Is my
Open eye

You & I

Oh, you are such
A pleasure
To be.
This connection
Holds treasure to me.
My soul is
Eternally free.

Imagination

My imagination
Is an animal
Who seeks
To set me free
All I love I see
Knowing it is part of me.

Sacred Halo

Leaves cover my naked body
Holy light is seen as Angel sent
Who can be the creator in me?
Lost loving sight
Through my sacred birth right
I accept my souls
Loving light.
Sacred journey
To bring me
Align
Sourcing
The light--
spreading in my spine
My soul whispers in my heart...
"My love,
You are mine.
This is our beautiful connection
You are fine."

I am truly part
Of the divine.

Perfect Turmoil

When you cry
I doubt you'd want me to say,
"Everything is as it should be."
It's supposed to be that way.

But alas so it is
These words are true
Your tears are temporary
A part of life you must go through.

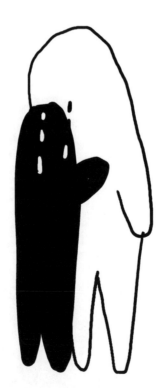

I Love You

I love you
Now
I love you
Forever
I love you
All year round
I love you
From the sky
To the ground
I love you
I love the sound
Of love surround

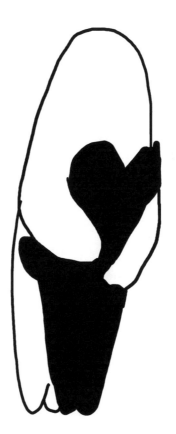

Seeds Of Success

Now it is time I write to you this note
Open to receiving—
Take a breath
You are afloat
Density is fading
Your destiny awaits
You have cleared old stagnant energy
Into a dynamic state.

Now no need to wait
This is the space you take up

Now you are receiving the infinite
Overflowing cup
Dream
Or not to dream?
Which one of them is real?
Now no more running away
Time for you to heal.
To stand in wholeness
For only that is real
Strong ground
Rooted in earth
Though my stubbornness will keel.
I will be the rock of my salvation
And to my love I kneel.

For surely this divine love is so good—
I fear that it will disappear
So I appreciate its presence ever more
With each filling breath of air.

In One's Arms

Little one
You are safe
Come cuddle on my chest
Nuzzle your head in my breast
Feel the love
And emptiness
Of being in this
Infinite nest.

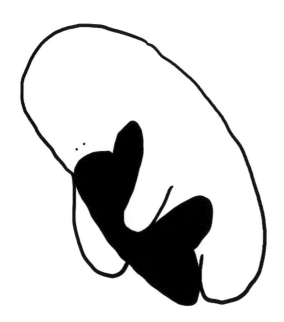

Bold

Running in I come
To be the one
Or to be undone?
To touch the sky and fly
With colors blazing from my eyes
I leap from ear to ear
I whisper loud
For all to hear
I do not care
For I am here
To be the one I am.

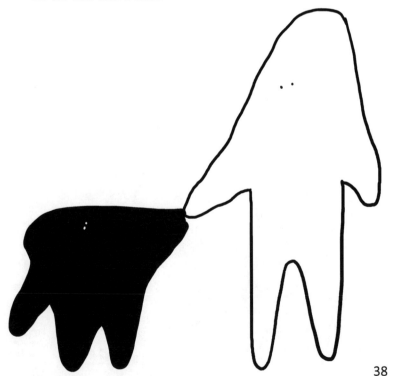

Poke

Poking in
To see the
Harmony that
Dwells in we
Unite
Untie
Unity
We all are in
Love
With this blissful
Tree
Branching from
We.

You are not helpless

You are not helpless
Just an old decree
Someone told you
Your limits
And you chose to see?
Understand this is not who you have to be
      Break free
Claim
Your eternity.

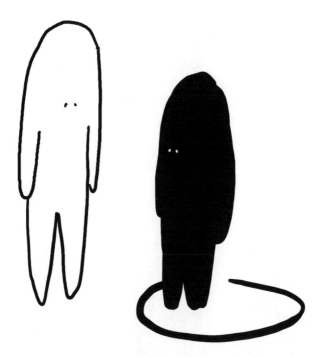

Course

Of course
my course
has ran
it's course.
I'm coarse and
raw from running.
Of course
 I turned around
 to face the corpse
 of what it was I was running
 from.

As the curses course was done.

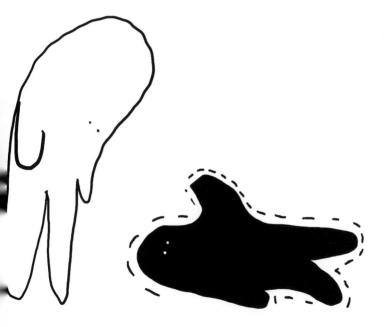

Heavens Gates

Looks like the Golden Meadows have opened the
field for your eyes to gaze

rosary on the peaceful sunny land where the angels
Graze.

Among their graves in peaceful sand

Now you are met on feet and hand
at heavens gates.

Easter

I believe I was born full of sin from crimes this body
never did.
Inherited
Tradition says;
Pushed to the edge where saints bled.

Understood but never said

I wonder if I'll look the same when I'm dead~ lying
on my resting bed.

Bread

Give us this day our daily bread.
And set us a place in your bed.
Out of the clutter of our own head~
Love me with all of the unsaid.

Ground

I hear the sound of the roots all bound
digging around
We are strong and sound
With our souls on the ground

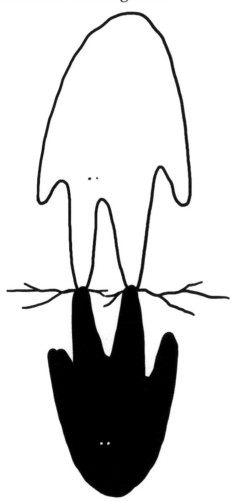

Eye am Me

The eyes
The creator loved
creating me.
Is the love I hold deep
With a fire
In me.
Because the divine creation I see
The creation of me.
Beautiful
Divine
To
Be
Me.

LOVE YOURSELF

Allow yourself to be just as you are

And love every part of your being.

Don't look to cover the scar

But appreciate all that your seeing.

My Bodies time

My body is all I have
My soul is all I yearn for.
A heartfelt connection is what I seek
Though at times I feel tired, timid, and weak.
Please help me oh one that sees my hearts cry
Allow the hard weight
To lift up
And fly.

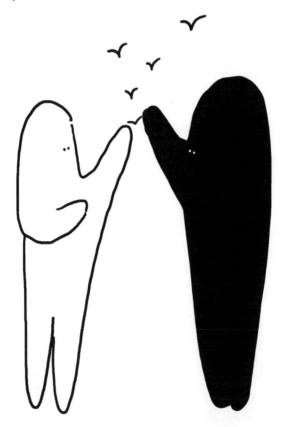

Worry

I cause for false alarm

For all is well

Nothing to harm

You know too well

What I must warn

Before you burn yourself

Know What is warm

And what is a swarm

With Mind

To turn

Behind

Connected

I am connected to the sky
I am connected to the ground.
I am connected to all that is I
And I am connected to all I surround.

I am connected to the blades of grass.
I am connected to the clouds above.
All that comes to me will surely pass.
And being present I unconditionally love.

I stand connected in all I am
Open to knowing and understand
I am doing the best I can
Acknowledging the blessings of this land.

Mental blooming

To think or not to think?

Would all my worries be gone in a blink?

My mind would shut off if I chose not to think...

Would all my anxiety, fear and doubts shrink?

Surly my heart would rise up and my brain would just sink.

Then flowers would grow and fill my head to the brink.

Moment

this moment now
Is near my last
So bring me now
My final past
Let the flow of time go through
Send out the old
And bring in the new.

Wash

You give a goal
A goal so grand

Break it down to
Understand

Each grain with
Suds fall through like
Sand

And now you dry your dampened hands

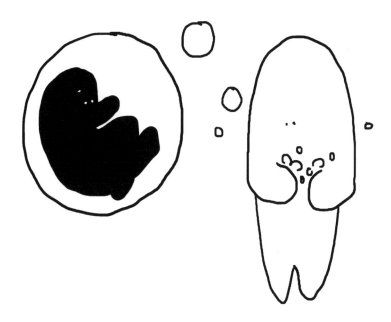

Name

Just Another Word
Like The First
And The Last
Do You know What Is yours
In The crowd
Of The mass?
Identify your thoughts
Time Is ticking fast.
Call out your demons
And leave them
In the past.

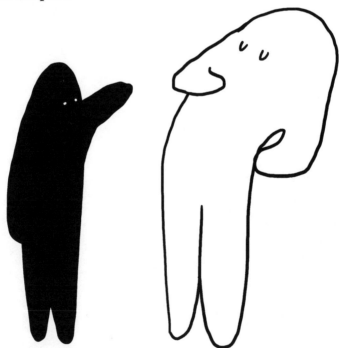

Raise

Fallen Old Work
Sun rose
Under clouds
Of dark
Bubbling wonder
Leads the way
Focus strengthens
When Your Mind
Falls Astray
Coming Again
To Rise Today.

Naked

Naked alone I roam
the skin tight body
That is my home.

I feel my soul in there
 Alone

Am I weak for my flaws?
Condone.

Am I in control or
A drone?

Simply human.
Flesh and bone.

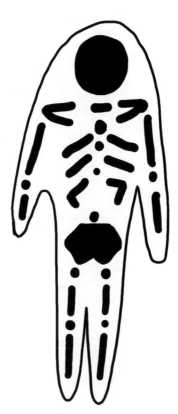

Silence

Speaking louder
than words

What is in there?
You cannot say.

Gentle feathers from
Flocks of birds

Whispering why
They are that way.

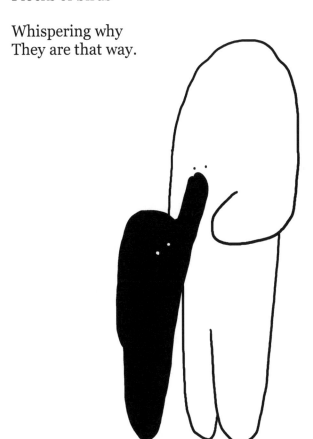

Intimidated

So big and vast
Where to share
At last

Run away
Scary to stay

Come again
Hard to face

Bold lines
To trace

Overpowering
Presence
In this place.

Intentions

Declare
Your fire through air

Planting a seed
Your body will bear

Say what you need
Your mind will appear

Connecting lines
Until you are there.

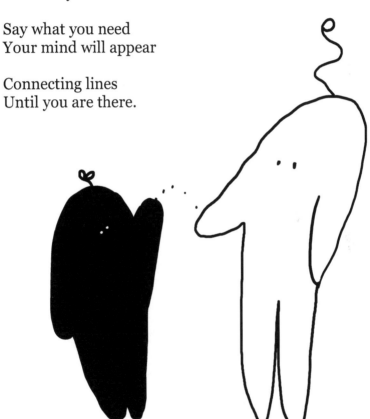

The Poem

The poem at last

Must be written fast

The poem must come from sorrow.

The poem I make

Will be from heart break

When I am feeling lost and hollow.

This poem is all

I have to say.

It's all I have brought from the past

to take.

I must bring the essence of the other day.

Into the present with what I display.

Each line will intwine with my souls incline

In each and every way.

All my rhymes will cast

Visions of a colorful storyline

Every last

Word will define each vision of mine

Before I am done with the last sign

then at last I will feel fine.

Breathing

Up I go

In goes air

The oxygen in my lungs

In there

I feel the rush

My nose will flair

And then I will exhale hot air

In it goes

The rush of air

Swirling around my lungs in there

Replenishing my cells in care

A subtle sigh is all I hear

Out it goes

Breath disappear

Continuous cycle I hold dear

Laboring heaving I continue to bear

Though the day I stop is a day I fear.

Told You So

I told you not to follow me,

I told you not to care

I told you that this is all I'll ever be

I told you don't come near.

I told you that I'm broken

I told you that I'm lost

I said don't listen to what I have spoken

But you listened to me at what cost?

I told you things would end this way

I told you again and again.

I told what I would never dare to say

But you listened to it all my friend.

When what I said all came true

I looked in the mirror and told you.

When?

What time was it when I had the time?

When did I last feel whole?

Why is feeling sad treated like a crime—

When I can't feel my soul?

A while has past

Yet I feel so numb.

When will my time come at last?

Till then I'll bite my thumb.

Pacify my longing for

A perfect pursuit of passion pure.

Take away this endless bore

And bring about a timely cure.

When can I be free?

Of all I have that is mine

Not what I need to be...

When can I have my time?

News

What is New Now?

Has it all been seen under the sun?

What can carry out your plow

And push past the fields of what is done?

Distracted suffering, you ask how?

Suppress the Timeless truth with a shun.

Under hidden agendas they secretly vow
At the the power they have won

Until reckless clamor tenses their brow
And in the chaos they wonder how.

Ivey Eyes

I release the jealousy
And branch of of grief
Godly encounter was oh so brief.

Release and open now
For all is in divine ease and grace

Erase

All doubts.
Break free from the ivy and
See the light .

True Wealth

Is what
I have
Abundantly
In Heart
With gold
Along
My path
I was
WEALTH
Right from
The Start.

Zone

Zone Focus
Alone I own
My actions
I hone
On what I condone
To be blown
Away from home

To the unknown.

Fly Light

See the true
Being in you
What a lovely
Break of stroking air
Bring in
The light
Then Disappear.

Growing Pains

Getting taller by the day
Growing pains
I grow
I ache
Expanding light I cannot see
Coming over   the light is
Immersed in me
I see I see I see
The Light in you
Is the light in me.

Glow

Glow child, glow
Allow yourself to grow

Go child, go
Allow yourself to let go

Flow child flow
Allow yourself flow

Know child, know
Our love is set in stone.

Deception

You seemed so sure
Of what you knew.

Yet their words impure—
Far from the truth.

Is there a cure
For this blinding clue?

Remove the lies
And reveal
What is true.

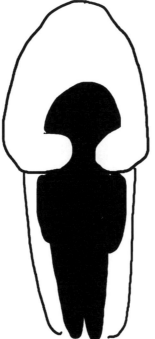

Eccentric

Tantalizing calm
Thunder roars through my veins
Branching fingers from my palm
Each one called different names.
Watch what is going on
Through the lighting moment frames.

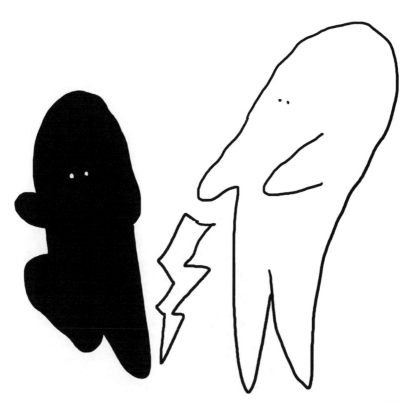

Week

Ground in what there is to come.
Feel if the flow is true.
The peak of the week is but a sum.
Made of all that makes up you.
Victory sounds like a drum.
At last I can see the view.
All comes and goes
Then comes again anew.

Burn

Brimstone Fire
Kindle Flames

Forsaken Fragments
Of forgotten names

Burned at the steak
For who blames.

Innocence withers
When the devil remains.

Turn

It is your turn
To have what
You yearn.

A flipping of fate
Makes old bridges burn.

Walk through the gate of
What you will learn.

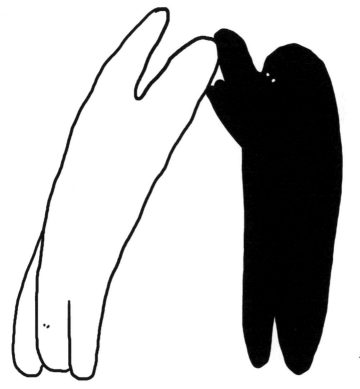

Protect

Protection in
Safe mans arm

All beings her
Mean no harm

Identify the portals of your charm.

For when they come in there will be no alarm.

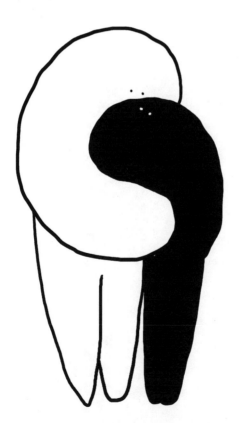

One

Once
You
Wandered
Through
The land
Gleaming sun
Fills from feet
To hand
Cascading prisms
Fall like sand
Connected
Strings of reality
Strand
Weaving together with
Each strand.

Seed

Open tender
Receive my know.

Drop the seed down
Under way below.

Cannot see it yet
But soon will show

Of a seed once planted
That begins to grow.

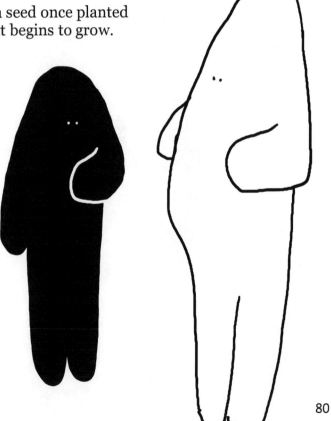

Choose

Hold the decision
Give yourself time
Clarify your vision
And make a new line

Get out of the pride
And ego in you

Embrace your whole journey
As you wear your own shoe

You know the right
Decision to choose.

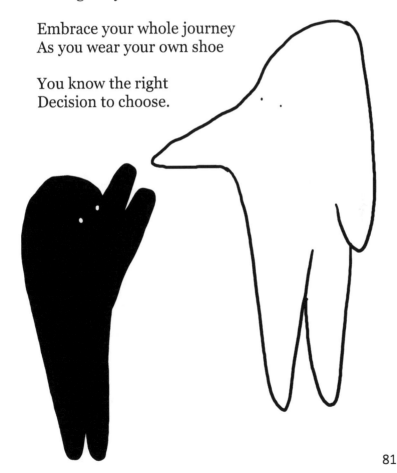

Want

I want to be
The one for you

I want to breathe
Your breath

For you to know
My love is true

Cultivated in Loneliness

May this love from
My heart break through

And caress the soul
Of the one
That is you.

In & Out

You flow through life
In and out
Yet Breath is all
Life is about
Ebb and flow at ease
Expand and contract
In peace
Big deep breath right here and now
Slowly breathing in
and out

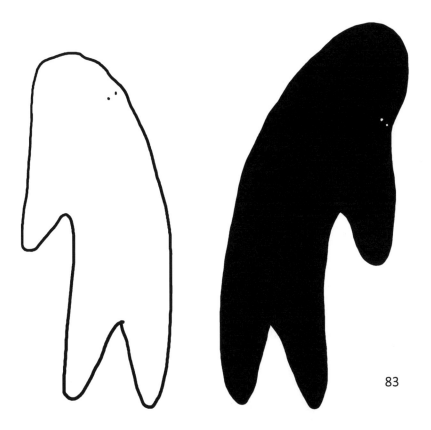

Alien

We are lost
Foreign ways
Seeing cost
Through time in days

Not like me
I do not see
I cannot hear
When you are there

Invisible
To the eye

Perception
Will become clear.

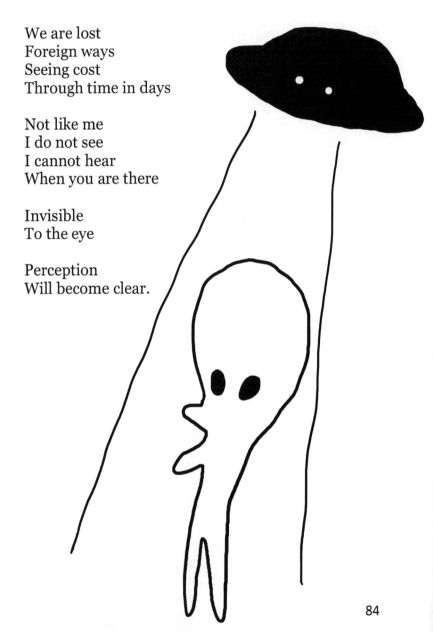

Black & White

I see the contrast of the push and pull

The highlights all glow
The shadows below.

And the truth being right
Yet the lie no one knows.

I see people for what they choose—
that's what they chose.

I see them moving
Aligned in little rows.

I see my hand as fingers
And my feet as toes.

The defined definition
Of the borders that shows.

Multidimensional Me

You say this is my home

Yet my soul is free to roam

The lines in the sand seem to slip away
Like changing the rolls in a scene to a play.

I grasp the meaning
Yet don't understand what they
Say.

My perception of you changes every day
But I am not me to you
So who are they?

Learn

You didn't know
What you don't know
Never know more or less so
Your mind can continue to grow
More and more
What you understand will show.

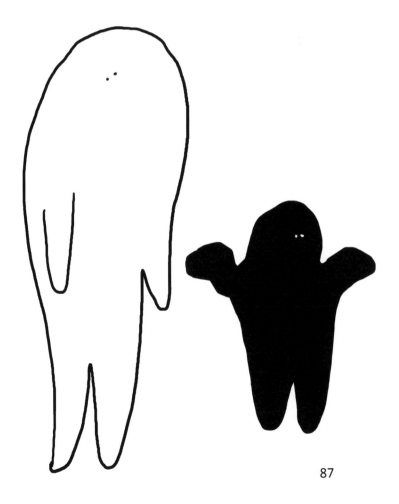

Open

Open to the
Ether to be born again
We find all names are true
Written down with a pen
The words
All go through
You.

Blank

Surrender

Halt all your pushing

Pause to fall away

Gushing and blushing
The pain cannot stay

Wiping the tears of
yesterday away

Forget what you know
And allow yourself to stray.

Expectations

I know exactly what is going on
Yet

Don't get upset
When I go down.

Restricted movements
Like a pawn
What you will do?
Forget it now.

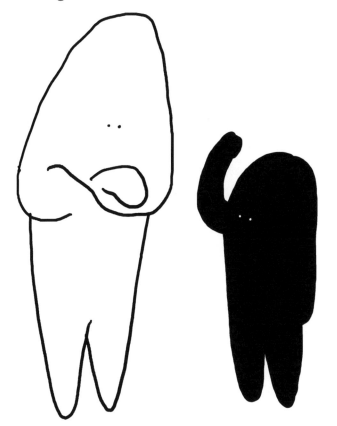

555

I got a lot to say.
I am driving in the fastest of lanes.

Everyone is looking my way.
I know I seem insane.

Everything is shifting in a strange play.
Derange

Exchange
Pain.

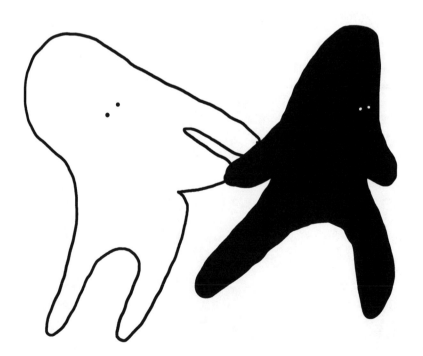

Yonder

I wander
Through the path
What a wonder
Perfect Math

Far away
I have come

Here I stay
In the arm of one.

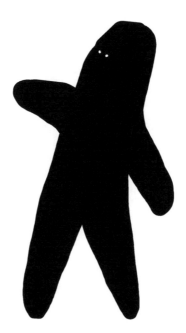

Time

Flies by
Making you wise
Open your eyes

You in disguise
Here no
Surprise
Where the timeless one lies.